*PERMANENT ADDRESS: NEW POEMS 1973-1980*

# PERMANENT ADDRESS

## *New Poems 1973-1980*

Ruth Whitman

ALICE JAMES BOOKS

ACKNOWLEDGEMENTS

Some of these poems first appeared in *The Agni Review, The American Poetry Review, Arion's Dolphin, The Beloit Poetry Journal,* The Bellevue Press, *The Bennington Review, The Boston University Journal, Counter/Measures, Green House, The Hudson River Anthology, The Massachusetts Review, Midstream, The New England Review, The Newport Review, New Letters, The New Republic, Ploughshares, Poetry Now, The Radcliffe Quarterly,* and *The Virginia Quarterly.*

*Library of Congress Catalogue Card Number 80-66182*
*ISBN 0-914086-30-8*

*Printed in the United States of America*

*book designed by Bruce Chandler*
*cover drawing by Morton Sacks*

*Typeset by Ed Hogan/Aspect Composition*

*The publication of this book was assisted by the Massachusetts Council on the Arts & Humanities*

Alice James Books
138 Mount Auburn Street
Cambridge, Massachusetts 02138

*for*

*Rachel*

*Leda*

*David*

# CONTENTS

HOLDING UP THE BRIDGE

Liftoff    *13*
Word    *14*
Arrow    *15*
Yom Kippur: Fasting    *17*
Soup Cools from the Edges First    *18*
Holding Up the Bridge    *19*
A Questionnaire    *21*


HUMAN GEOGRAPHY

Seven Variations for Robert Schumann    *24*
Bubba Esther, 1888    *31*
My Greatgreatuncle the Archbishop    *32*
Maria Olt    *34*
The Language of Hills    *36*
The Grilled Window, Jerusalem    *38*
Mediterranean    *39*
Human Geography    *41*
Watching the Sun Rise Over Mount Zion    *42*

## IN THE COUNTRY OF THE WHITETHROATED SPARROW

In the Country of the Whitethroated Sparrow     *44*
A Phoenix     *50*
After     *51*
Apple     *52*
Fog     *53*

## ROOMS OF THE OCEAN

Rooms of the Ocean
  *crossing Tiverton bridge to Aquidneck Island     56*
  *Second Beach     57*
  *Bishop Berkeley's Rock, Middletown, R.I.     58*
  *yellow     60*
  *Purgatory Chasm     61*
  *the moon over the sea     62*
  *August storm     63*
  *Sachuest Point     64*
  *a veil fell just now     67*
  *December sunset     68*
  *the beach in winter     69*
  *the light the face gives off     70*
Singing     *71*

# HOLDING UP THE BRIDGE

# LIFTOFF

You will make a myth
out of the ordinary
rising beyond your skin
into a new country

         breaking the thin
         filaments of gravity

You cannot elevate
without the hand of wind.
The strong
air stalls in your lungs.

         You hesitate
         on the brink of land.

And in this instant all
the sorrows of obstacle
pause and dissolve.
You lift—

         and, barely moving, skim
         the impossible sky.

# WORD

A fur muscle ran across the road.


Only when I saw the pointed tip of it
waving, did I think *chipmunk*.


Sometimes we move inside our bodies
as inside a stranger.  The sack
hangs loose, inviting us to think
*I can be anyone, go anywhere, do anything.*


But once your pen touches paper, all
choices become one, the word as single
as the chipmunk moving in one spasm
from green to *green*.

# ARROW

*The aiming:*

you aim at the center of the eye
you gather all landscape around that single point:
    if a bird-ribbon flies across the edge
    if a cloud teases the sun
you gather all to the one point

there is only one


*The letting go:*

you are let go
you are no longer grasped
empty air surrounds you

you no longer lean against the bow
your hock is free
you are free
you are in danger
remember the center

all of you remembers the center


*The flight:*

you are moving along an invisible track
(you make it yourself)
straight as your spine is straight

you move forward
air whistles past you
you are speeding towards

      you are gathered
      you are pointed
      you are free
      you are in danger

the center
of your eye

## YOM KIPPUR: FASTING

The appetite
stirs.  On this one day
of the new year
the head becomes light,

without embroideries
of tongue or hand.
Saliva drying, your body
is a transparent cave.

You can see
through the skull into the brain's cavity.
You are a harp for whatever wind
God wants to play.

His music sounds sharper.  There is no
barrier between his thought and you.

# SOUP COOLS FROM THE EDGES FIRST

Here's the only praise
you can give yourself:
words will obey

you if you listen to them, let
patterns emerge. Otherwise,
nothing will come out as well

as you wish it. Except, when eyes
are not watching, there will rise
deep explosions of joy

from the middle of the earth,
in the dark, mind you,
where the heat still lies.

# HOLDING UP THE BRIDGE

The diver under the bay
reports the concrete block
holding up the bridge
is cracked and crumbling.


A narrow road
arches over the water space,
dips towards the shore.
One end of the bridge
goes down on its knees.
Cars and trucks
tumble off like toys.


No.


The diver is lying. Inside
that concrete block
my bones
are holding up the bridge.


> *Three times the builder tried*
> *without the sacrifice,*
> *three times the bridge*
> *shuddered and collapsed.*

*And then he knew:*
*only the bones*
*of his young wife*
*could placate the girders.*


*She came, bringing his lunch, singing,*
*the birds warned her:*
*that was at Arta,*
*hundreds of years ago.*

# A QUESTIONNAIRE

*Describe your early education.*

At six, standing on the low stone wall
beside my grandfather, I was taller than he.
Wearing my white beret, hair cut short,
with leather leggings to my knee, I put my hand
on his shoulder possessively
and sang him his lullaby, *a moloch veynt,*
an angel weeps, an angel weeps.

*What is your permanent address.*

A flat rock in Central Park
where an innocent policeman
found me with my first sweetheart.
Under Cambridge clocks chiming each quarter hour.
Beside the sea.
Beneath Mount Zion.
On Boston's broad Victorian bosom.
Across the pond where you are standing, laughing at me.

*Male or female.*

Both.  When I saw the Greek Hermaphrodite
I recognized myself and you, each
two in one.  Now I know why
the Masai warriors grow brave
by drinking blood and milk.

*Are you married.*

> Yes, many times.
> I marry my first loves
> over and over. Like coming home.

*Describe a crucial event in your life.*

> At twenty, I died and was born again. For a while
> I died every day. One day when I was dying
> beside the sea, which ignored me,
> when my guts ran empty and I started sinking
> into that bottomless hollow
> beneath the bed, I suddenly heard
> (through the window, in my head)
> the notes of the *Appassionata*
> calling me back into the world.

*List your awards and honors.*

> Three children.
> One, a yellow tearose.
> Two, a winedark peony.
> Three, a young fox, heart's desire.

*Give a brief statement of your plans.*

> To fly.
> To swim across the pond.
> To tell what I know.
> To love you harder.

# HUMAN GEOGRAPHY

# SEVEN VARIATIONS FOR ROBERT SCHUMANN

1.

I want to explain about the broken finger.
It is all appetite.
Voracious, exuberant, world-
devouring appetite.


When I was five
they found me at dawn beside the piano
playing chords and weeping.
Even when they boxed my ears
for putting a thumb on a black key
it did not diminish my appetite.


I used to place the music
upside-down on the music stand
and laugh at the strange intertwinings
like upside-down palaces
reflected in the canals of Venice.
The notes stare at you
with strange eyes—eyes of
basilisks flowers peacocks maidens.


At twenty, determined to be a virtuoso,
I knew I must risk stretching myself
to the snapping point.


I made a pulley to strengthen
and stretch my hand.

The pulley held one finger up
while the rest played.
I heard the finger snap. I thought
the pain would make me faint. Vertigo.
A crippled pianist.


Who will attempt to reassemble the burst bud?


2.

My mother called music The Breadless Art.


It was my ring finger.


Little Clara, fifteen, eyes enormous
in her delicate face,
played Hummel for me. It was as though
champagne flowed from her fingers. She stroked
my hand, told me not to drink too much beer,
not to turn day into night,
and to write to her.


I write letters of the alphabet
only under compulsion:
I find my real language
in sonatas and symphonies.

She is my hands. My A-major.


I'll fill a balloon with my thoughts
and send it by a kind wind: I'll harness
the butterflies
to dance my two-sided soul to her.


And Clara in answer
will play my new Etudes, saying
she knows no other way
of showing me her inmost heart.
She dares not do it in secret
so she does it in public.


A kiss on the stairway.
A blue dress.


### 3.

I had a dream of walking beside a deep pool.
I threw my ring into it,
then suddenly longed to fling myself in too.


The need to write is so great,
if I were on a lonely island
in the middle of the sea,
I couldn't stop.

When I published my Opus One,
I felt as proud as the Doge of Venice
when he married the sea—
I now for the first time
married the whole world.


When I wrote my Spring Symphony
my state was like a young mother
who has just been delivered—
light and happy
yet sick and sore.


Clara—now woman, wife, mother, mine—
finds me sometimes very grave.
But I do not allow her to watch me
or practice her piano
when I am composing


4.

There is a ringing a kettledrumming a trumpeting
inside my head.  Heights beckon me,
they want me to jump,
sharp knives terrify me, death is on every side.


Only at night, shored against Clara's sweet body,
now full with our third child,
does the raft stop rocking.

5
Silence.


                   I cannot lift my arm
to conduct.  The players before me
seem far away.
I see them
through veils and dim windows.
Their instruments
are crumbling to dust
like old newspapers.


In Venice they asked Clara, after her concert,
"And is your husband, too, musical?"


I hear one note constantly in my head,
one single merciless note,
tuned to A.


They told me a young man had come to call.
Thin, shy, he sat down to play for me.
At once I knew—a genius, a young eagle.
I called Clara to come and hear him.
This is Johannes, I said,
he is the one
I have been waiting for.


Clara is pregnant with our eighth.

6

The single note is opening like a flower,
a melody of petals in E-flat major
whispered to me by Mendelssohn, Schubert,
they want me to write it down,
                              no,
                                    the angelic voices
now have the faces of tigers, hyenas
who want me dead, who want me dead—


                    It is raining, it is Carnival,
the ring finger, the ring, I must
throw it into the Rhine, I am sinking beneath
the green mystery, I hear
the secret music.


7

Locked in this safe place
I sit in the cool garden
making lists
of German towns and cities.


                    It is two years
since I have seen my Clara.


                    It is hard
to move my tongue.  Or hands.
But now she is sitting beside me and she

is lovely.  I would like
to give her a flower.  Or a butterfly.


Brahms is standing behind her.
She is pouring me a glass of wine
and offers it, her hand shaking.
A few drops of wine
spill on her hand.
I lick the drops from her fingers.

## BUBBA ESTHER, 1888

She was still upset,
she wanted to tell me,
she kept remembering
his terrible hands:

> how she came, a young girl
> of seventeen, a freckled
> fairskinned Jew from Kovno
> to Hamburg with her uncle
> and stayed in an old house
> and waited while he bought
> the steamship tickets
> so they could sail to America

> and how he came into her room
> sat down on the bed, touched
> her waist, took her by the
> breast, said for a kiss
> she could have her ticket,
> her skirts were rumpled, her
> petticoat torn, his teeth were
> broken, his breath full of
> onions, she was ashamed

still ashamed, lying
eighty years later
in the hospital bed,
trying to tell me,
trembling, weeping with anger

The cossacks snatched him from his mother
at the age of five
to serve in the Tsar's army.

He was farmed with a family
who found him so docile, so bright
they forced him to enter the church.

One day he passed through the shtetl
where he was born, Borisov,
and he heard the sound of a melody,

mournful and familiar.
It haunted him, why was he so shaken by it?
He grew up and became an archbishop.

In the middle of a foursquare
Gregorian chant
he wept to remember

the old Hassidic notes:
di-dona-di, di-dona-di.
They drew him back, back to Borisov,

to the house of his kidnapping.
I am the brother of Yitzie Orkos, he said,
I have heard of my nephew, Yankev Leyb

(that was my grandfather),
he too wants to be enlightened, he has
secretly taught himself Russian,

let me take him, let me educate him:
I have no children of my own.
But they refused,

they denied him,
they were afraid.
It was the time of pogroms.

What was a Russian Orthodox archbishop
doing in their Jewish house?
They sent him away.

## MARIA OLT

On a hillside in Jerusalem
under the hammer sun, she lifts

a little carob tree, the tree of John
the Baptist, and sets it

into its hole. Solid as a house,
she is called Righteous, a Christian

who hid Jews in Hungary. Her hair clings
around her broad face as she bends

with the hoe, carefully heaping the soil
around the roots. She builds a rim of dirt

on the downhill side and pours water from
the heavy bucket. She waits until the earth

sucks the water up, then pours again
with a slow wrist. The workmen

sent to help her, stand aside, helpless.
She straightens up. Her eyes are wet.

Tears come to her easily.
The small Jewish woman she saved

stands beside her, dryeyed.
Thirtyfive years ago, as they watched

the death train pass, faces and hands
silent between the slats, the girl

had cried, I want to go with them!
No, said Maria, you must understand,

if you go, I will go with you.

# THE LANGUAGE OF HILLS

The slope of that hill
is saying something to me,
something diagonal, stony as music.

What is it saying?

*Horse.*

A bony horse
is grazing on its lip,
white bones on tufted brown.

Does it say *sheep*?

Sheep like stones?  No,
but a shepherd moves restlessly
across its haunch.

It says something else:

*Weight.*
*Sky.*
It hoists an old city on its spine.

Now I hear:


Trash spills down its shoulder,
bullets, blood,
kicking up the tan dust.


I stumble among the stones,
hearing
*footsteps.*

# THE GRILLED WINDOW, JERUSALEM

Beyond the grilled window:
yellow suns on a bush,
churchly cypresses, mud, rosy stone,
a tower that talks to angels.


On this side:
books, spoiled paper,
tongueless lectures. Hatshepsut
is finally at peace with her
double sex. The Persian lovers
twine around each other.


Radiance leaks through
the diamond-shaped spaces.


I'm on both sides
preparing
to walk on the ancient hills.

# MEDITERRANEAN

### 1

The sun is a gold coin slipping into
an envelope of sea.

### 2

The sea is a mouth
that opens at the horizon.
Everything in the sky
falls into her.

### 3

She is hungry for the first fruit
of evening.
She draws him into her,
a round harvest.

### 4

She is swallowing
an orange.
She is sucking it in
slowly,
whole.

### 5

He slips down her throat,
a pocket of fragrance.
His orchards burst open.

6

Tomorrow he will rise
crescent by crescent
above the dusky hills.


7

A saffron air washes his absence.

The mother rock is black basalt,
hard, handsome.
Walls are made of it, ancient
synagogues, the house of
Saint Peter's mother-in-law.

Climatic conditions:
a rush of new milk,
brief rains, the slow
grinding of wheat,
disappointments.

Bits of rock fall.
Each passing heel
grinds them.  They are whipped
by the chamsin, dried
to fecund dust.

From this my children rose.
They were crops, they were trees.
They will squeeze
greengold liquor from olives
ripening by the black wall.

# WATCHING THE SUN RISE OVER MOUNT ZION

Orange fish are swimming
over the roofs.

The air is tinseled
with scales of gold.

Someone is coming.

All the harps cymbals violins
drums horns cellos
sing
     one blinding note.

The tower is on fire.

It is today.

# IN THE COUNTRY OF THE
# WHITETHROATED SPARROW

1

two long calls
and three triplets
from a sky of blueberry blue


now   now
it is now   it is now   it is now


on an emerald division of earth
we two have come
to a halfmown field


lying circled with pine
we breathe with a sharp first breath
new hay   clover   sun on bark


and the whitethroated sparrow
two-thirds through our harvest
cries   now   now   it is

2

    over the darkening harvest
the sky curves heavy
    with silent birds


we come from a room
    secure in lamplight
where a trio of Schubert


    waterfalls us
into the shaking thunder
    long hands of lightning


reach over the pines
    thrust above the meadow
and weave us garlands


    behind us Schubert sings
over stones glinting through
    great sheets of light, it is now

3

A million kilovolts eat
the dark. We're inside
an electric gale,
watching the white


bones of trees appear
and disappear. The night
is flying metal,
each piece a radiance


of stones, grass, the pillars
of the porch. The neon
sky cracks on and off,
blowing me like wind


against your mouth,
where I am struck to ash.

4

Time is the mountain that watches over the meadow.
Circling the loved shape in a wedding dance,
we look for a path in thickets of maidenhair,


assault the pinnacle blazed clean by fire,
stretch our lungs in unaccustomed air,
climb across rocks, streambeds, logs,


past trees in second growth, up granite slabs,
muscles in back and thighs reaching
to take the moment, ratify the day.


Breathless above the stunted trees,
above the tangle looking out towards valleys
of promises, somewhere in the pines


below (but seeming high above), we hear
a voice speak prophecy, the sparrow sings
plainly in sheets of light over the peak


not   yet   it will be   it will be   it will be
nudging us gently down, where we must live.
Time is the mountain bending over us.

5

spaces of sun and shadow
are painted on the grass
again
unlooked for
the season of harvest
in the play of light and morning
your loved shape
moving towards me
through the trees
almost rounding the path
renewed there
coming coming almost
here
the pines dark with longing

6

a stretto of birdsong:
one cry scissors the air

across the dawn
a crow hones his call

on the granite sky:
two one-notes

echo each other
question and answer

rapid as rain falling:
a cricket adds his bass viol

and the whitethroated sparrow
hidden in pines

waiting for sun
to zigzag through leaves

lets drop half his song
two long calls and a pause

# A PHOENIX

When the embers have fallen away,
she turns towards him—

against all
expectation,

all design,—
holding time

between her breasts.
How does he know

he is being watched?
By the silence?

By a change in the air
behind him?

He thinks something hostile
bristles the hair on his neck,

but it is she
from an empty beach

parting the air
around him.

## AFTER

The sand was tender,
motherwarm to my feet,

the cleft in the rocks
dazzled my eyes with absence:

the sun pressed down, and the sea
as it rocked in my arms

shamed language
and the language of comfort.

## APPLE

Love, on your grave—flat
and strange in the dry grass—
I place a stalk
of red and yellow
everlasting
and prop it
beside your name.

Apple, you called me,
thinking of a girl
round and succulent,
thinking of pink and white
petals blowing their honey
breath over us
that first nuptial summer.

Tomorrow I will bring you
small Rhode Island Greenings,
new red Macintosh
to moisten
your dry sleep.

# FOG

SHE                    HE

I come to your shore longing

                you don't notice

for the shape the rise of your land

                how sunlight sieves

your special rounds and levels

                through me   you come

but you pull your blanket over your head

                a large shape

hoping I will think you

                that parts and breaks

all flat all gray

                my brooding   you are

a separated mist

                all troubling

no shore no trees no sky no water

                waterfall

you pretend that you never

                all whirlpool

tugged me under your cover

                you don't see

or drew me down to your contours

                how I become lost

that you never entered my crevices my

                in you

long cave and shook me

        you are final

back to my beginnings

        I am germinal

you hide from me

        stop moving

pretending to be blank

        rest in me

look at me

# ROOMS OF THE OCEAN

# ROOMS OF THE OCEAN

*crossing Tiverton bridge to Aquidneck Island*

where the Sakonnet river becomes the sea
a flank of water
stretches pewter to the horizon


the morning sun has sucked the sky white
leaving below a blanched gray disk


under the bridge
the river curves northward,
stained a deep irrational blue


I come to the edge where the island begins


a strip of silver foil
a dagger of ocean
glints just beyond Saint George's tower

*Second Beach*

once on your edge
in your adolescent embrace
I read my summer hunger

I brought my loves to you
one by one
testing them against

your indifference you
my first love and my last
still hiding your secrets

*Bishop Berkeley's Rock, Middletown, R.I.*


A natural sphinx—
head and shoulders—
thrusts out of the landscape
and stares at the great bowl of ocean before it:


its jaws, once filled with soft soapstone,
have been pried ajar by time:
                              in that maw
where timothy grass grows in puddingstone,
Bishop Berkeley sat, where you and I


are sitting now:
                    we climbed up, as he did,
through tangles of cat-brier (the long talons
trying to hold us back),
through thickets of blackberry:


we sit in the mouth of the sphinx,
looking down over wild pear trees, wild black cherry,
over feathery locust buckthorn, over the half circle
of farm and ocean that makes the world:


the Bishop sat, musing on Reality,
waiting for sails to bring
King George's gold for his Academy:
but the sails never came:

we sit cradled in the lion's jaw,
imagining sails, surveying
the promising false horizon:
behind us dwarf ebony spleenwort

clings to the roof,
blackstemmed fern growing against gravity,
against all nature, nourished by
random drops of rain, reflected light:

beneath us the rock is a palette
of orange and black patches, strange colors in a cave:
spiders hold their kingdom here, weaving their traps
from the upper jaw to the lower, undisturbed

*yellow*

the sun lowering through the porch windows
rinses everything I look at with little suns
the metallic skin of the ocean
the western air opening wide
reels me into its yellow mouth
as it swallows the rocker, the book
I am reading, the watery golden panes

*Purgatory Chasm*

a deep cleft
in a cliff of puddingstone:
once a stripe of quartz between boulders
cracked open when the sleeping ocean
shifted: the surf
nagged out the rift
splinter by splinter


into this breech
two Puritan lovers leapt
(the legend says),
hand in hopeless hand:
and a suitor jumped across,
dared by his mocking mistress:
black prints in the stone
prove the devil once passed by


now boys and girls climb down
between the lips
to gather rosehips
or sit reading on a steep
shelf in the sun
or stand on a rump of rock
watching the sea
boil in the abyss

*the moon over the sea*

still brightens the flesh of
lovers, still sets them in
a magic country, still
makes a myth of their brief
gestures: their bodies are
wiser than their minds: they
climb up the ladder of
the moonlight, then let go,
spill themselves into the
buoyant the shining flood

*August storm*

the gulls are
breasting
a southeast gale

the wind holds back
their weight
with its palm

stiff winged
they stand
on the wild air

resting against
the wall of wind
rain

is starting to fall
staining
the waves

slate gray and white
foghorns of autumn
begin

*Sachuest Point*


on this small tongue of land
shaped by the surf
where the Sakonnet river
merges with the sea


a salt water farmer
built his house
two hundred years ago:
his windbeaten meadow


lay covered with timothy
dwarf trees
bent to the blow
steady from the southwest:


here on the lip
of the continent
his neighbors were wind and stars
birds and field mice

    \*

generations
passed across his fields:
in nineteen fortyone

the warring world
made this spit of earth
a target base


soldiers drove their trucks
over the timothy
piled cement blocks


strung barbed wire
across the rocks and grass:
but we climbed


around the beach
slipped past
the target range


and swam in our secret cove
naked
to the sound of guns

    *

after thirtyfive years
fat shadows of owls

glide over the meadow
over crumbled cement,

over shards of glass:
flocks of scoters

ducks geese
rest in the coves

dancing the cadence
of their long migrations

their bed
of spindrift

moves with the pulse
of the open ocean:

the farmhouse stands
blind

its face turned
to the sea wind

*a veil fell just now*

between me and the white ocean

one of the shutters of evening is closing

the blind hands of tides
are feeling their way
below the cliffs and mountains
beneath the forest of water among
the weeds and eyeless fish
along twilight canyons to the

underside of light

*December sunset*


the room is blinded with sunlight
burning silver foil pingpongs off
the ocean the sun already
past its zenith the surf busy
flooding and unflooding the curved
beach   the north wind catches the spray
and hurls it towards the open fetch
of sea   my sun about to set
but first I'll send fingers of light
to outline the clouds caress the
firepool over its basalt bed

*the beach in winter*

in this round gray February afternoon
a dish of silver tilts into my lap

along the edge
I trace the stiff

white lace
where spindrift

lifted up
and froze

*the light the face gives off*

your aura
when the sun bounces against you
gives me back a sea of flints

even under the shadow
of dwindling boulders
you fling me shimmering nets

without the sun
without the white relief
of your breaking

in night's unclosing eye
I know your face is gathering
is gathering its light again

# SINGING

### 1

three spears of sunlight
lay across the floor

each stream of pointed brass
pierced her throat

### 2

she built a tower with her voice

it grew upward
until flocks of chimney swifts
flew in and out of its arches

### 3

twelve sandpipers
skittered behind the long lip
of the tide,
pecked at the seaweed:

then skittered back
up the beach
legs trilling
just beyond the wave's bite

### 4

sailors rose through her voice
from their drowned boats
drifting up
through the sharp blue of her throat

2/9/9
gift

### 5

a chorus of gulls
turned and wheeled
over the full-lunged sea:

the sea sang
basso profundo

it had no doors

### 6

they sang together:

she moved
breast first
across the curve of the globe

she arched over
the hidden geography
of the ocean floor

she sailed across
its peaks and resonant valleys

singing